Little Houses

Sundress Publications • Knoxville, TN

ISBN: 978-1-951979-39-3
Library of Congress: 2022945145
Published by Sundress Publications
www.sundresspublications.com

Book Editor: Erin Elizabeth Smith
Managing Editor: Tennison Black
Editorial Assistant: Kanika Lawton
Editorial Interns: Fox Auslander, Emily DeYoung, and Nicole Bethune Winters.

Colophon: This book is set in Adobe Caslon Pro.

Cover Image: "Unititled" by Reem Alathari

Cover Design: Kristen Ton

Book Design: Erin Elizabeth Smith

Author Photo: Leticia Andrade

Little Houses

Athena Nassar

Acknowledgements

Versions of these poems have appeared previously in the following literary magazines and anthologies:

Academy of American Poets: "Alligator"
Atlas Magazine: "Mouthful of Orange"
The Bitchin' Kitsch: "the performance"
The Chattahoochee Review: "Georgia bleeds"
DIALOGIST: "metamorphosis"
Infection House: "Afternoon Tea with God," "where the flies hover II"
Lake Effect: "Little Houses"
The McNeese Review: "Dinoflagellates"
The Missouri Review: "Avareh"
New Orleans Review: "vignettes of a lost wife"
Riggwelter: "ghost girl(s)"
Salt Hill Journal: "athena as princess peach"
San Miguel Writers' Conference: "so i let you be a canvas"
Southern Humanities Review: "Ken-ya See Us Now"
Sport Literate: "Flight Drill"
Sukoon: "The Fallen Mango II"
Up the Staircase Quarterly: "Coming of Age"
Zone 3: "Little Boy as a House with Big Windows"

"Alligator" won the 2021 Academy of American Poets College Prize.

"Afternoon Tea with God" has been republished in the 2021 Greater Boston Intercollegiate Poetry Festival Chapbook.

"so i let you be a canvas" won the 2021 San Miguel Writers' Conference Writing Contest.

"Ken-ya See Us Now" was selected as a finalist for the 2021 Auburn Witness Poetry Prize.

Table of Contents

PROLOGUE

Alligator

To your lover, you say swallow me whole. To the world,
   you say come dip your ladles in my fertile belly. The well
is always full. The water is always warm where the sun

beats down. I say you should cry where nobody will
   hear you. On the bank where I am pulling you out of its
mouth, I am clutching you by your legs, each leg

kicking back as if a part of you wants to stay wedged
   in the throat of what will kill you. On the surface where
it hovers, I find you, mouth impregnated with

pomegranate, juice streaming down your chin like
   a punctured artery. The earth waits to open and drag
you under. Pray for him, then leave him buried

in the house with the holes in the walls. In the belly
   of his own outrage. Close your mouth; the world will never
lift a glass to your dry, wrinkled lips. No one will ever

love you like you do. I pray you will emerge from its
   throat, wet and awake and gasping for air. It is not your
lover. It is not your enemy. It is you, stranded in a body

of freshwater, feeding on your own hunger to please.

I. HOUSE OF GOD(S)

Avareh

for Dairy

Outside the urgent care, we sit like crescent moons dropped
from the sky, our bodies hunched over the sidewalk. Down here
with everything so up close, we can see the people, holograms

of themselves, pushing through each other on the street, droplets
of water falling past them, oranges toppling out of brown paper bags.
Gravity is something even the moon cannot control.

I turn to you, your mother and brother fallen with the droplets
and the oranges, and think, what do I know about grief? I know
the sun was punctured before light came pouring from it

like the yolk of a runny egg. I know I wake some mornings
with the fear of my mother dying too soon, the thought a bird
I must shoo away again and again. I wonder how you

shoo them, your many hands flying in every direction.
These birds, immigrant children, like us. Look at how the moon
glows a blood orange with all the fruit that fell in it,

all the mothers who populate the sky. I watch the swinging
doors of the urgent care and ask myself, *what good does it do
to worry about my own?* Will it slow my mother's descent

if I hold her, like a brown paper bag, from underneath?
In Arabic, we have five ways of saying *okay—Tayyeb. Tamaam.
Hasanan. Zein. Mneeh.* My mouth attempts to pronounce

this shared language of acceptance, but the word *hasanan*
sticks to the back of my throat like a grain of rice. I'm scared
to tell you I never did like leaving, fleeing one place

to populate another. Your mother country calls these people
avareh, longing souls, their feet at the edge of a well to another
country, a puddle of souls floating belly up. They see

themselves in this puddle, but they also see themselves
in the droplets yet to fall in, happy tears of God spilling like fat
melons from somewhere above us. I want to pry them

open, swish their many seeds in my mouth. I want to tell you
I'm scared of waking up. My heart, a bird batting its wings to go
nowhere. My mother, a sound lodged in my throat.

Little Houses

We walk in and out of little houses, and I pretend
the bonds between state and people do not concern
me. I have no friends in the whole state

of Georgia. And if I could, I would disown
the state itself. (Surely, if it hadn't disowned me
first.) In the art history museum, I point

at pretty paintings that I cannot touch or blend
into, but only admire, mashallah. (God bless it.)
Is it God who has willed me to be so detached

from men, or my own state of unwillingness?
If I were to sculpt a state of my own, it would be
called The Province of Vagiña, assuming

it hasn't already been colonized by some
Anglo-Saxon European monarchy. As mixed girls,
we are forever stuck in between little houses.

Little bathrooms with little mirrors and a man
waiting for his turn, but wouldn't it be indulgent
to stay awhile? To sit in the middle of two brush

strokes without being claimed by The Province
of Purple? Van Gogh fed on yellow paint in fits
of anxiety, however, I lock myself inside

infinity rooms. In light of God's will, I split
into microscopic versions of an abstract Egypt
to go down easier. There were no portraits

of Arab girls in the Post-Impressionist era,
but if there were, her eyes would weep honey
so rich that it would dare the painter

himself to crave yellow. She would be hung
on the walls of some aristocrat's estate down South,
and she would hate it there. To manifest

is to walk in and out of little houses and pretend
you built them. To pray for a kaleidoscope of gods
and hope one of them is you.

Afternoon Tea with God

God invites me to a weeping willow to apologize for those
he took from me over a cup of tea. I am inclined to accept

this proposal, because quite frankly, I have no prior
engagements, and the world is too pale to be fickle.

At five o'clock, we sip tea on a branch in the sky. I nibble
on blueberry scones and watch the crumbs falling below,

as if I can't fall with them. When the wind blows,
fine china rattles, and the antique silverware of God

shakes in my grip. My flesh proves to be nothing but
an overskirt for my bones. My bones, but an overskirt

for my spirit. We take another sip and exhale into
another hour. Another day where we eat above those

below. Though God rubs the glaze from my cheeks,
I am not aware I am being fed. I do not question who

placed me on this branch when I am six stories high.
Too high to smell the bodies, so I smell chamomile

instead. God's fingers are an herbal hallucinogenic,
a smooth gloss brushed over the unholy. I cannot see

the people who lie on the grass. I cannot see the people
who lie. I take one sip closer to the day my flesh

will be blown far away from my bones. Spirits rise off
the steam from our tea, and we absorb them.

Ken-ya See Us Now

2017 Super Bowl

I am a housefly floating in a cold glass of milk.
I am at a friend's house watching the game.

Her grandfather points at the players swarming
around the ball, says, *negroes shouldn't git tattoos,*

can't see-um anyway, his Southern drawl savoring
the E in *negroes.* His recliner, a throne made

of cotton. I don't tell him about the Ancient
Egyptians stenciling blue symbols into their flesh

before the punk rock bands made it popular.
The painted people in أبيدوس [1] carving gods

onto their stomachs to protect their unborn
children. We were branding ourselves long before

the boats came. We were branding ourselves
millenniums before the cop brought the weight

of his knee, a hot iron, to brand a Black neck.
It is half time, and I am thinking about

what my folks are doing. What I want to say is:
At my house, we watch basketball. We eat

---

[1] Abydos, Egypt.

whole racks of lamb and wash them down
with whole milk. We eat. We take up   space.

We support Black and shit. Instead, I say:
Good game.

Not Because They Love Me

The more I love a thing, the more I want to invade it.
As a child, I would take my mother's hair, slick as the black
eggs of a beluga fish, pressing it to my cheek, twisting

it until it broke from her scalp. To bless myself, I drink
from the well until the stones hold no water, and my belly
is a cold lake. The horseflies feed on my legs not

because they love me, but because I am a body of blood.
On the floor of the Red Sea, my ancestors lie beside the reins
of their horses. On the floor of my body, chariots lie

under my veins that once pulled horses. I have been
the colonized and the colonizer. I have been kissed, my lips
parting for the oars of tongues, while countries are being

fled. Before my father left Cairo, he gutted the trees
of their olives. Each time I leave home, I make spoons
of my hands and spear them into the bucket of rice

my mother keeps by the window. There are always deer
outside, their backs peppered with white spots. The many
eyes of God waiting with their lids peeled back.

My Judgment Day

don't you have any morals
left to flock around your   naked body in the grass
like turkey vultures   their cluster of heads   kidney bean red
their eyes   little tomatoes don't you have any   morals
left to eat you   and eat you   to hang you up on
the cross and feast   their eyes on   your flushed face
on your head hung low don't you   have any grief left
to beat you while you cry   out to the Heavenly Father
His palms pink   from beating you   don't you have any
mothers left   to bathe you in an ocean   of cleanliness
in a hot spring   of sweat pooling   in a pressure cooker
of gods   don't you forgive   yourself for the nights
with the men draped   around your back like sheepskin
the men hung   like curtains that   open for you
don't you   enjoy yourself as you live   in one night
and another   as you inhale the day and hold it
in your lungs   two swollen dates on the verge of   bursting
out of your chest if   the day is   a vineyard you are
the crusher   of grapes your bare feet   bleeding wine
your mouth bleeding   a full and round   laugh leaking
into the night   air thicker than kissing   thighs much
darker than heaven   much sweeter than the fruit
jammed between   your toes   don't you have any shame
a stampede   of hooves to crush   you they   crush you

II. HOUSE OF TEMPTATION

ghost girls

It does not matter where we are going
when we look like this
Floating like pollen over Boston sidewalks We like when they stare
Our perfume carrying
with the breeze
We glide past streetlights
hollow homes hollow
boys Their vital organs gouged out with a spoon and folded neatly
in a plastic bag
I pass through them because I am the breeze
bottled in a plastic shape
In knee high boots I pass
through train stations swing on metal poles
until I lurch forward
Forward is the only way we are pulled
to the party where the boy waits
We speak in hushed whispers inhale the perfume on our wrists
until we are filled with one another's scent
We smell like a bouquet
of youth
and the hollow men breathe us in

at the party where he takes my hand
passes through the bodies
rocking like a current
It does not matter where we are going
when we drift as ghosts of ourselves blended into each other

We evaporate into the bodies
drunk on adrenaline
on their own self obsessions
They mirror one another

arms thrown over their heads in worship
His body relaxes into mine
and I wonder what it's like to be consumed
to be lived in like a beehive
and savored like honeycomb
I have lost the others in the swarm
of my obsessions
I wear him like jewelry
melt him down and slip him around my neck
for family dinners weddings christmas parties
carry him in a burlap sack like my vital organs
In the end we bleed the same
when I peel back his layers
to reveal a skeleton of a scholar

He is still dancing
and I have already passed through him.

the performance

someone wishes me a blessed solar return, and later that night
i blow out my candles, little wisps of smoke dancing around
the puffed up soufflé. sometimes, i wish to be the man in the strip
club with his hands behind his head or rather, the woman popping
her perfectly round ass against his lap, a big ass planet orbiting
to the beat of Megan Thee Stallion singing *body-ody-ody-ody-ody*.
i wonder what it would feel like to undress myself to that kind
of praise, to squat naked in the center of someone's universe
and say *don't touch*. on the streets of paris, the woman they called
the Hottentot Venus was purchased by a man who showcased her
beside a rhinoceros. those who passed would gawk at her full
body draped in ostrich feathers, stick their hands through the cage
to squeeze the fat on her hips. they pulled at her brown flesh
as if she had the thick hide of the rhinoceros itself. she did not
get to undress herself. this was done by the men who paid to strip
her of her feathers. i do not wear feathers. when i give myself
to someone, i am the one who gives myself back. when i blow
out my candles, everyone sitting wide-eyed around the table,
there's a part of me that wishes to light them and blow them
out, just to light them again. after the applause, i drag the knife
through the soufflé and pull it out, custard dripping from the blade.

The Brunch Girls

sip blood orange cosmos through skinny glasses,
careful not to fall in. They are from a place

you've never been in the Middle East. They are from
the outskirts of Atlanta. They ask for a table

on the patio to be seen. The brunch girls are bored
of you and craving a bacon, egg, & cheese

sandwich. Last night, you dreamt of the brunch
girls kissing you all at once. Of course this didn't

happen! The brunch girls are kissing you with one
mouth and the hand of God with the other. He is

watching from that table over there. The brunch girls
read Immanuel Kant when they are not giggling

about their exes butchering the word *foie gras*.
Immanuel Kant had a previous commitment

to the Enlightenment of self-centered men long
before the brunch girls. Everybody else scrambles

to be enlightened. They drink coffee with cream
to camouflage the coffee. They crack pepper

onto their omelettes and say *what did you put
in this?* as they feed it to their dog under the table.

Everybody else is a bunch of liars for their own
good, but the brunch girls didn't need to tell you this.

No Free Milk

We are placing banana slices on nutella toast, my friend's blond, chunky hair falling around her face like strips of the peel. I enjoy telling her about my sexual escapades with college boys. Really, there haven't been many, so I tend to recycle certain stories for her amusement. Some boys were fun, but there are some I regret (I don't tell her those stories). As I'm licking the gooey residue from the banana off my fingers, she asks me again about the first boy, the Swedish one from Harvard.

By now, Mom has made her way to the coffeemaker. My dad, still in his underwear, strolls into the kitchen. He grabs for a mug and says, *oh yea, that was just a one-night stand. Remember Athena, no free milk.* I imagine myself as some drug-induced cow lying belly up, a line of breeders waiting at my udders with empty cups. My dad looks at me as if I have a yellow tag on my ear that reads *breedable.*

Mom attempts, in clipped whispers, to chastise Dad. She takes another sip of her coffee and tells him, *you really don't think before you speak; she's going to be judged.* He apologizes, laughs. I wipe a fat tear off my face and finish my breakfast in silence. I realize my dad might always see me like this, desperate cow crying into toast.

2.

The other morning, I heard my dad telling my mother, *your body is mine.* Maybe he thinks that's what happens when girls share their bodies. He thinks boys take them and never give them back. Mom, propped up on her elbow in bed, brushed her hand over her hips and replied, *no, my body is mine, and your body is yours.* Grabbing for her hands, he said, *we are each other's,* but I know he does not want to be owned.

athena as the Garden of Eden

don't bite into a pineapple if its succulent scent clings to your taste buds the sticky sweet dew drips into your core but the juice is sour on the tongue i know there is a boy throwing parts of you into the Persian Gulf because i put him there his skin crisp to the touch *is this too sweet? someone pinch me* you kneel on grains of salt as he cups his hand over your mouth muffling the sound of hand-me-down cries swallowed butter has gone rancid cutting the insides of your cheeks pineapple slices dripping acid onto the roof of your mouth you prick your finger trying to peel the rind you always did all the talking insect guts spill out of his sour center that once had a succulent scent a soup of black beetles and fleas don't run before he walks *i told you* i set a steaming plate of barbed chicken wire in front of you check inside before sinking your teeth into your tropical tombstone there may be a boneyard under your feet.

the invisible man

I.

something about the way my mother's grand
piano appears when i am not fully awake how it hangs
in the center of the room
like a dead man
a three-legged silhouette casts an ugly shadow suspended
over a spiral staircase i watch the piano lurking blink
blink again and float
up the staircase as the piano follows
heavily behind it leaves a trail of mud
tracked in from outside frozen on the staircase
something is brewing in the dark the canvas never painted on
the loveseat never sunken into
the antique lamp unplugged from its socket
someone watches
us from the window and laughs
because i forgot to lock the front door
stupid girl
i am ashamed of my stillness
try to plant my feet in the staircase i blink
and see the piano slowly moving closer
eyes growing heavier

until everything is black

II.

the sun leaks in through the blinds, all of its orange
light making orange rivers

on our faces. with our wet bodies caught
together, he says, *this is how you lift your hips*

to mine. caught between gum and bone
i find myself drowning in a mouth

that isn't my own. my own tongue is an eel
that has been coughed up, nocturnal thing

prodding blind. my first kiss is a whole bucket of eels
poured into my belly, all of them prodding

to find a way out. when his mother gets home,
she offers to make me fried egg rolls.

his stepdad smokes outside where his red truck
is parked, his mouth bleeding clouds

like exhaust from an engine. the mosquitos cling
to the damp patches on his white undershirt.

i drive home in the dark, the headlights
shutting on. my body navigating back to itself.

III.

something intimate
    a cold breeze leaking in from outside

the bathtub   a sound like a washing machine
    orbiting   the faucet drooling a bubbly paste

i see in streaks of color   in cherry red pop rocks
    and this is how he comes to me

his cherry red tongue slides down my vertebrae
    the bathtub is lit by only   a flickering lightbulb

that casts a shadow on the wall   he begs me
    to turn around into his arms

the thick arms of the bathroom slowly shrinking
    he begs me to squint   to truly see him

his bones rattle against the porcelain bathtub
    color slowly leaks

through me   i wince when i hear him moan
    his harsh cries absorbed

into the tiles, into my bare back
    bent down in the bathwater   he blows on my neck

with cherry red bubbles   his face a black cherry
    he begs me to see him

IV.

bathwater spills out into an ocean
in the middle of nowhere.
in the heart of the unknown,
it is too dark to see below.

Mouthful of Orange

My hand pokes through the hole in the wire fence
to pluck honeysuckle from its roots. The orange petals

leak creamsicle to coat my lips. I ignore the woman
when she tells me to step away from the fence.

My hands bleeding chlorophyll, I peel back the membrane
of a mouthwatering dream to suck dry the nectar.

I dream of a girl who makes herself a boat with white
sails. The sails are bowls of wind, and they take her

to the orchard where the sun beats down on the
honeysuckle. The fruit of my land was made to spill

from the cracks in my fingers. The land, like fruit,
was made to fill my bowl too. Beyond the fence,

the women gather in clusters like poison oak. They lay
their cold hands on my shoulders and spread an omen

in the form of a pink rash. Slurping the milk that pours
from the petal's tear ducts, I do not listen when they

tell me what is mine to drink and what is not. My back,
as if bombarded by raspberries, oozes blisters.

I continue to eat away at the flowers, not knowing
and not caring whether I am awake.

athena as strawberry jello

A boy who resembles a man asks me *do you know how much*
a jello shot costs? He slurs his t's, and I try to solve his words
like a crossword puzzle, and it's only 6 p.m. I row my way
through a sea of red solo cups and fake IDs from South

Carolina, Arkansas, Florida. Faces don't match the pictures, but
the bartender doesn't know 17 from 21 when he puts bass in his
voice. When girls wear their mother's shoes, they are still girls.
When I click my heels against the grass, they don't make

a sound. Young Thug spits into his microphone. His lyrics have
gone stale like an old dinosaur fossil, and I taste dust on my lips
when I inhale. I learn not to inhale when I walk through thick
smoke. It tastes like cucumber and mango and skunk on my

tongue. *Is this what freedom tastes like?* I can't reach my arms
out without feeling the weight of sweat drip from his back. He
asks me to dance, but I can only read his lips through the bass,
and I don't want to dance through a cemetery for crushed solo

cups and spoiled spirits. I take off my heels and sink my toes
into the wet grass stained with strawberry jello. I bounce like
jello through a crowd of strangers I've known since kindergarten.
Their faces blend into the moon when they are all stomping on

crumpled tickets. Toilet paper. Broken heels. Water bottles. Pennies.
Pumping their fists to the dust that hits the wind. Even my own
name sounds stale when I say it over and over. Cardi B makes
a surprise appearance. Cardi B   Cardi B   Cardi B. She's 8

months pregnant with a baby who shouldn't be inhaling cucumber
smoke from kids who told their parents they were sleeping over at

a friend's house. My parents know where I am, but my face doesn't look 21, and I can't breathe with the weight of his sweat on my chest.

III. HOUSE OF THE SOUTH

Georgia bleeds

red mud quick and narrow like a stream—an artery that cannot be corked. Trucks wear Confederate flags like a slip dress in the summertime, and I laugh, because it makes me think of my grandmother's hijab pulled tight around her skinny face. The flags, spitting out little drops of blood, breeze by the paved streets of I-85. So Georgia is bleeding, but nobody cares enough to run cold water on its incisions or at least pray for a quick and painless death. Heat runs through my blood, dry like Egypt's narrow streets or the irritably hot winter. Suburbia is a blue flame I cannot stomp out with the bottom of my shoe. It is not an ant hill. It is not a monarchy. There is no queen of (*insert boring street name*). They do not bear the wounded on their backs like saints if it isn't Sunday. They attend church services, their skin sun-dipped in spray tans. In sun hats, they lick sugar from the rim of lemon drop martinis. Heaven is a members-only country club with grilled chicken kebabs in mint yogurt and roz bil sheraya and no entrance for Arab girls.

vignettes of a lost wife

I.

It is April. Climbing roses crown headfirst through
the soil, ripening under my crisscrossed legs

without permission. The aroma of apricots hangs
in the air like wet linens, tempting the noses

of churchgoing boys, but I refuse to let Georgia's
thick heat crawl up my spine. I bury my face

like a plum in the picnic basket. Embed my irregular
heart underground where the dead things lie

unbeating. Under a willow tree, two men swap
tongues. Their bodies knot together like garden

snakes unaware of my presence. They breathe
from the same lungs. From my picnic blanket,

I count people in pairs. Pair myself with the wind
and blow in through someone's back window.

I appear like a love letter sealed with hot wax.
My skin smells like comfort food, so I let them

eat me. They draw me in and fold me like linens.
Wear my hands around their backs and scrub me

until I am clean. I lie on the grass with an empty
picnic basket and count the church-going boys.

II.

My partner doesn't know how to count, and it is
apparent in the way his feet trail behind him

like a stubborn child. How his dress shoes, like knives,
carve my toes each time we spin around.

He is a different partner. One who counts well
and blends into my dress made of red satin.

I smother him in red, paint his neck with lipstick
and show off my legs when he asks for a new

partner. I meet one drenched in a blue suit. In tears,
he rocks to the music. Eyes wallow in my satin

skin, but I am not the one he wants. To be used
is to dance with a man being pulled. To ignore

the tugs on his chest. A string puppet, I rise for a new
partner. Rest my wooden chin on another chest

until it rises to the moon where I once danced.
Debutantes tripping on my scattered pearls.

On calloused feet, I limp to a new partner made
of stone. His hands leave cement on my shoulders,

so I stand cemented next to him. Next to me,
he is a monument I fear will come crashing.

Come rushing like an avalanche into my arms.
I try to gather the shattered cement without

carving my fingertips. Longing for another piece
of the monument, I brush myself off for a new partner.

III.

Hooves blow down the track, light as the gust of air
that kisses my neck. The man in my ear whispers,

the remains of candy apple still in his breath. I crave
the crunch of his cinnamon shell in my teeth.

The thoroughbred kicks dust to the breeze like cinnamon
and gallops past me, body lifting from the ground.

His rider, lifting, yanks at the reins. Feels the ground
when they land. Hooves buckling, saddle slapping

the back of the thoroughbred. Weak from the sun,
I fan my powdered face and enjoy the pleasures

of the pure-blooded. Skin rich as caramel, groomed
to be rich. To run from the horses' tongues flying,

teeth grinding for my ribbon. The man in my ear
speaks a smooth tongue, listens for the downbeat

of my drum. His candy apple lips swollen with dollar
bills. He wants to be chased. To be loved by a marching

band. The thoroughbred reaches the finish line,
tears through the ribbon. His heart pounding

against his ribs like drumsticks. His rider slaps him
on the back. Runs his fingers through the mane

drenched in sweat and waves the medal in the air.
High to catch the spit of the horses' tongues flying.

IV.

We throw him a party with red velvet cupcakes.
Children flying from swing sets like pterodactyls

screeching through the backyard. On the terrace,
we sway, admiring our fruit swelling with age.

His cheeks coated in globs of red velvet icing,
skin glazed in caramel. He is four years older today.

Cuts our hearts in fours as we watch him grow
older. We hang onto time, talons snagging onto

his cheeks, hoping to reverse the years fed
piecemeal to pterodactyls. Their mouths always

hungry for Halloween candy, bubblegum, baby
teeth. We swim through his old candy wrappers.

His letters are never-ending paper cuts opened
and reopened. Ruptured eggshells, his father

and I are prehistoric monuments not meant to
survive the test of time. Aged by butterfly kisses

and children weeping. Their pretend sadness worn
like a fur coat. Like actors, we cater to their fake

papercuts, kiss their fingers when we are bleeding.

Coming of Age

tonight i eat my dog in a fever dream
the internet says i'm too young to have a heart so i forgive
myself for the slaughter i let her outside
for too long i search for her somewhere between my house
and the river where the dead fish lie belly up a heart
should be there beating
just under the water running with blue
flesh i do not claim to be humane
in the coming-of-age film
where i bite off my mother's hand and grow into
a better woman after i swallow the hand
i blame the mouth for its hunger
i blame the dog for running
tonight the river begs to feed on the marrow
of some wild animal its throat blue with transparency
with smaller rivers with little tongues lapping
at my feet the internet says a dream is runoff
from a past life i stick my arm into the stream and pull
out the meat of the world thrashing its cold body against
my wet face before slipping back into the stream
nobody told me how to stop the crying after the push
i grow tired of looking for the living in the mouth
of the dead so i return to my house without the dog
tuck my tail between my legs and ask for another dog
one with brown spots and no teeth promise
i won't let her slip down into the river this time
only this time i sleep tonight my dog scratching at the door

where the flies hover

I have diagnosed my father with oppositional defiant disorder,
a rather genetic condition. His symptoms became clear

on the last day of summer when a heat wave oozed
through Georgia's sugary casing. My brother, too, was surprised

by my revelation, because ironically, he has it as well.
If you choose to dissect a mango, first you must bear down

on its stringy flesh. It is my last summer as a fruitless girl.
The summer where I will hatch from my shell

of a home, while my mother so eagerly tries to duct tape
my disembodied embryo. It is a quiet day on the creek.

My family has spontaneously decided to go on a hike,
an odyssey of sorts to unclothe what already lies naked

in the center of the woods. I am turned over to reveal the gut
of my exhaustion, smothered in pine needles and sweetgum

seeds. The most menacing tumor of the suburbs. This is
where the flies hover over my father, where he will feed

on ambrosia and never leave. For we went one way, and
he went another, lured deep into the stomach of the woods.

where the flies hover II

(an elaboration of the diagnosis)

I am a lover of all things defiant in nature, including
my father's need to disobey. It is the summer of the pandemic

and a dull summer for us all. I have not contacted the friends
I have left in Georgia, because I have made the conscious

decision not to. The news tells us the pandemic is a hoax.
The news tells us there are 63,000 cases in Georgia. Cameras

pan over the beach like little flying robots that attach
to disaster. In this case, disaster is a chili lime margarita

and drunk people swimming in their own sickness. The news
tells us to stay in our houses. My father, upon seeing the news,

decides we must throw ourselves into this public showing
of defiance that reporters call disaster. He rents a beach house

with beach chairs and umbrellas. He makes his family an
umbrella and spreads us in the sun. Four Arabs walk on a beach,

and little cameras attach to us. I am photographed in a pink
bikini on my last living day. My father tells me to cover up

for live television, but I am immune to the bugs that live on
the beach, and after all, I am defiant in nature. Like other girls,

I set up a camera of my own to document my body, pink
and exposed, in a global crisis.

After the Song

in memoriam of Brigit Pegeen Kelly

The goat's head has stopped its singing. The boy
who hacked it off is now a man, but when he kisses
his child goodnight, he still sees the goat's eyes,

like halved peaches, peeking above the sheets.
Some of our crimes cut most when they stop singing.
Some of our wounds bleed out when we forget

what did the cutting. All of us have a goat head
hanging in the hollow part of our chests. We mourn
for the body that was not inhabited by the head.

We mourn for the body that did not tell us we are
gutted fruit. Bone sucked of its marrow. Headless goat
thrashing its hooves in a shallow pond. Some

of us will succumb to the thrashing, our lungs slick
like blue stones, but most of us will stop flailing and float.
Sheets of ice split off from what we were before.

The Study of *Look at Me*

I return to the French Quarter, because it makes me feel
as if I've washed up on the shore of an independent film
with English subtitles
where nobody is ashamed of their bodies
and people smoke pipes on their terrace.

I wonder if it is possible to be so attracted to one state
and so disturbed by my own, but then I agree,
we come to hate the things that reject us.

I think of my grandmother urging me to write my ABC's
with my right hand
before slapping my left,
her need to correct my most defining trait.

I think of the old
and stubborn DVD

that scratches on the most poignant scene.
But I must admit, I am a lover of all things
defiant in nature.

There is an artist who paints on naked girls
in the Quarter. He has a debilitating eye condition
that runs in his family,

keratoconus,
I think.

But I am captivated by the irony of an artist
who cannot see. Nevertheless, he has chosen the study
of *look at me*

which attempts to correct him
in his blindness.

There is a part of me that wishes to give him my back
as a canvas, and there is another that wishes to slap the hand
that holds the brush.

He paints a girl black and hides her in front of a black door.
He paints a girl a door and calls her *Equinox*.

Because he cannot know a day
without the breast

of night
itching to be seen.

IV. HOUSE OF TECHNOLOGY

athena as princess peach

i find myself
wedged
between mario and bowser. afraid
my pretty pink gown will snag
on his shell decorated
with teeth from girls
like me. girls that don't have toads
to wish upon. i am a girl
whose crown has been mauled
by a kitchen blender. vision blurred by pixels.
he presses y and i dive into a piranha plant. i don't ask why
through my pink lipstick. lips sealed shut. is it wrong to be
a girl who screams *finish him?* i wasn't programmed to jump
from the back balcony
into the moat. my manual doesn't give me instructions to escape
through pipes, flying turtles, jewelry meant to weigh me down
into the blades. i can't freeze
the vines that wrap around my pearls
so tight. super mario feeds me grapes
to keep me entertained. bowser dips my hair in lava
to see how far i'll go—

Call of Duty: The Only Female Character Gets Married

LEVEL 00: PICK YOUR PLAYER

I am a human who needs
but I am not needy
I do not crave mornings
with dogs and lawnmowers
bodies sealed together by the paste
of their sweat   I swallow
defeat in small increments   tucking it behind
my tongue to spit out
and flush down the toilet when no one
is looking
I chop off the hand
that pats my head
as a shovel pats dirt into the field
watered by weeping girls

(It is done with garden shears.)

Weaknesses: N/A.

LEVEL 01: WAIT. . .

My opponent is choosing his player
somewhere behind a computer screen.

(He clicks the drop-down menu.)

Hair color: Brown.
Eye color: Brown.

His hair is thick like the night that comes after a heavy rain and his lashes are long black feathers.

He selects a fancy watch.
He selects some kind of explosive.
He hits play.

LEVEL 02: WAR

I bury myself in the hollow space in the meadow.
It is behind a red shed.

I bury myself poorly
on purpose.
(He finds me.)

I am abandoned in the apocalypse where collar bones
were sucked
then eaten.
There are no players left. We get married.

I prepare for another battle—
soak my feet in the blood
of weeping girls.

I cry into my ammunition. I reload.
My toes dig deeper into the mud
wet with rainwater.
The ground is grotesque when it weeps.

LEVEL 03: I DID NOT WANT TO GET MARRIED

My loud cries wake the dead.
Zombie intestines splash onto my face.

I pry open the mouth wrapped tight

around my finger, choked blue. Engaged
and disengaged.
Oxygen is for the unwanted.

LEVEL 04: RELOAD…AGAIN

My opponent pours hot soup
down my throat.

I cry. I buffer. I—
clean the memory card.

athena as villanelle

i find myself
on a couch cuddling
with a Russian diplomat   i plan to blow him
up
when our TV show is over
or on a commercial break
nobody could've seen this coming—me
a babe with a bangin' body
igniting the big bang in   his body
a Russian diplomat imploding
a galaxy caving in on itself
in the face of a woman
who matters   pile of matter in my hands
a cold-blooded collector
of broken men   of silent bombs
nobody heard the   heart attacks
in the sky before they saw
a downpour   of light
of female gods coming
to bless or debone
them with their bedazzled wands   to carve
their organs   in pig masks and tulle skirts
every man
i touch turns to   powder   every body
i enter turns   flammable

athena as telephone operator

I sit in a hotel pool to absorb chlorine, to let wires wrinkle
like dried fruit. I am a prune, unstoned
untouched.
This is she, scalp smothered in a crushed velvet hat. In a telephone box
of a dress, I sit crushing cigarettes. A spectator

of orchestral music, of diatribe at continental breakfast. A woman
with too many capers on her plate yaps at a waiter.

Her voice scratches through the speaker like cat claws
on a grand piano.
HELLO?
I stuff my mouth with sugar cubes, so I won't have to answer
the woman on the other end. Her cries are porcelain cups
crashing

onto white cloth tabletops. Into pools, I dive to unplug
from the other end. My breaths are text bubbles.
I escape the box, where my back would shrivel downward
listening.

Where cigarette smoke would hang in the air like legato notes.
I stay under until my lungs are sealed
shut like ziploc bags.

I cannot bring myself to pinch the cords binding me
to the other end. I must be connected to something more
than a dial tone.

When I lift myself out of the water, cold streams rushing
down my face, I remind them:

I'm listening. Please hold while I connect
you to—I mustn't lose myself. Please—are you still there—

Colonization as Sci-Fi

I like to believe my father is a member of a suburban cult
made of middle-aged men. They all smoke foreign cigars

and talk politics as if the government isn't one white man
pouring acrylic paint on the window

of an artificially lit greenhouse. The TV is turned to some
kind of sports channel to give them something to watch

or drool over, and I can't help but notice them from a distance,
gathered around the TV like livestock. Then I remember

the time my uncle said *we are all living in a dystopia
of sorts.* Of course, my uncle is a walking conspiracy

theory, but I picture this: A table full of George Orwells
choking on jalapeño poppers. A realm where children

slip into television screens and are never seen again until
year 3000. What I didn't know is that my uncle meant

something much darker: They'll burn a cross on your yard
if they don't want you in that small town in Florida.

I look at my father and wonder how many crosses he has
burning for him in this small town brimming with livestock,

people with pitchforks waiting for us to leave. I am treading
on a breeding ground for want and a hotbox for consumption.

Perhaps this is why I ate fluorescent lights as a child.
Not to glow, but to conquer the glowing.

V. HOUSE OF THE ADOLESCENT

Dinoflagellates

I was only three when my aunt, the cultural anthropologist, whispered stories in my ear before bed. She left out the guy I met at that Christmas party, Jonathan. God collects men with J names and scatters them amongst the seven continents to eat at us all. She told tales of belly dancers jingling coins on their hips, temples worn down to skeletons. Of demigod children, Scylla and Charybdis, creatures that bend to the hands of little girls like me. I was little, thin as a celery stick. Looked up at the other girls who looked down to me. Down the bioluminescent bay I soared, petting dinoflagellates and watching how they smile at me. Their teeth neon. Lying on knotted rope, my body a tug of war between countries. The palms of my hands, a yellow cream like the sesame seeds my grandmother crushes for tahini. My veins green like the olives my mother pours into Spanish rice. I observed the other girls, how their hips didn't jingle. Their bodies ripe plantains that had been picked too soon. I didn't want to be picked, so I ran from the men who picked us. Didn't stop running until I washed up on the shore of some man-made island and my aunt lying there in a hammock. Told me to get a drink.

On Parenting

My father can't let him know he's afraid.
He removes the door from its hinges.

My brother is a door with no hinges.
My father unplugs the gaming console.

The game, to fire bullets with no console.
They wound one another outside the screen.

I've seen their wounds, my face a black screen.
Pinning his hands, my mother chokes on her cries.

Like mothers, cardinals gag on their own cry.
Raising a boy is not like raising a bird.

When you raise a boy, you become a bird.
What you become swallows what you were before.

My father swallows what he was before.
He can't let him know he is afraid.

Flight Drill

then the old man in the front row stands up to yell *TRASH!*
his Sixers jersey dripping with diamond chains, and the cameraman
cuts to him waving a t-shirt in the air, spit flying out

of his foamy mouth like confetti, and my brother misses it all,
his baby blue headphones noise canceling the knife-like bird calls
of the old man, of the stadium singing, of life dribbling

all around him. last night I dreamt of a ghost standing
over us, then I became the ghost hunched over him yelling *EAT!*
little wisps of spit flying out of my ghoulish mouth,

and I mama-birded him the whole earth spinning on
its tilted axis, its atmosphere inflated with freshly pumped air,
and now the old man puffs out his chest, hollers *BOO!*

at the Hawks, their broad wings sprouting from their
muscular backs, their feet lifting off the court as if the earth
was thrown from its axis and is now plummeting

to the bottom of the universe, and I turn to my brother,
his head bowed down in another universe, and I tell him when
you've always flown so high, everything, including you,

appears to be falling—the Sixers fans, a chorus of birds
echoing one another's call, and the referees, the directors
of the choir, blowing on their whistles as if they

can stop themselves from falling, and then there is you
with your baby blue headphones, unaware you are floating
over the stadium like some kind of hip-hop god, but

this is not the end of the world. this is you sitting courtside
at the playoff game of life, the one I had to fight you to attend,
and covering your ears from the dribble.

Monochrome

I am at a birthday sleepover that my mother forced me
to go to. It is raining and irritably dark for August.

I don't mind. I've grown to like the deficiency of color—
learned to limit myself to one color a week. This week,

it is purple like the rain beetles that infest our homes.
The undertones in the birthday girl's face yelling at her

mother to take the cake out of the fridge. Her bedroom
is crawling with pink, a malnourished version of purple.

I already want to leave. Crawl under the wallpaper and
stay there until one of the girls decides to peel back

my fuchsia skin. Since when do we glamorize the color
of our tongues? Since when do we feed cake to girls

who yell at their mothers—celebrate their birthdays
as if the world wasn't coughed on with a cornflower

blue the day they were born. Still, we all sit in a circle
on her carpet, trying to shake the powder from our hair.

We agree to play sardines, and I do nothing at all when
one of us is locked in the closet. Instead, I celebrate

the birthday girl's barbaric wishes. I celebrate, because I
am not locked in her closet, buried in the birthday girl's

pink wardrobe. I count to twenty and soak into the carpet
of rain beetles, drown out my conscience with laughter.

Overwhelmed with seasickness, I am too much of the
birthday girl, my eyes glazed over with magenta.

The Fallen Mango

When the mango falls into the crowd of careless girls
they gawk
at the piece of fruit like one of those kids
from the nineties juice commercials
captivated by the orange blob thrown in front of them
until they grow
bored. Numb to the things that are given,
the girls pour soda over the fruit flies
to watch their little legs squirm and crawl
over each other. Under the setting
sun, the girls pick at other girls
while the mango browns
and their mothers worry about where they are.
They do not blacken their spirits with definitions
of selfish
because they have yet to grow
into themselves
and no time to worry about the fallen.
Full-bodied mangoes drop from their chests
when they turn thirteen
and they are too young to ignore the old man
who tells them they're pretty
enough to sell.
It is not until time cakes onto their stomachs
that they learn
the life of a mango waits for no child
wasting away from the inside
out until all that is left
is the sorry
spoiled pit.

The Fallen Mango II

When my father says *mangoes are the nectar of Egypt*
I imagine him
searching through the desert with his two brothers
carrying jugs of water on his back
and picking the heads off of scarab beetles
until he finds the perfect mango
and squeezes all of the pulp
into his dry mouth. I imagine
my father as a child
riding his bike
through Khan el-Khalili,
talking to a street vendor
in a language I do not understand
because it is in his blood
to bargain
for the prettiest mangoes.
My mother says she used to climb thirty feet
for the juiciest ones
and throw them down to her five siblings
under the tree
like a cluster of hungry birds.
But when I imagine hunger
I see a mango falling
out of the sky,
a crowd of children
who have already eaten.

The Day We Lured the Moths

As children, we buried ourselves in boscage cypress green
like our bruises. Hung bed sheets over moss beds crawling
with cicadas humming like when our mother folds laundry.
She wasn't outside the day we lured the moths with cheap beer,
waited for the molasses to melt into their abdomens. How
fortunate we were to watch our muses marinate in their
drunkenness, curling into one other. My face eclipsing
yours, I taught you how to hold their brittle wings
in your hands. How to preserve yourself with citrus
when I wasn't outside. Even I couldn't leave the labyrinths
we built out of cardboard, avocado peels, dish cloth wrung out
and hung to drip dry as if it were never defiled by dirty hands,
blackened with char-colored blemishes. Our mother's body was
a fertilized flower pot. We had poked our eyes through the holes in
the ultraviolet sheets to see her watered and glowing and full. She
would rock us in her arms and pray we caramelize and ripen
like squash set to bake. You used to stutter, your tongue bent
iron, before you were chosen—plucked from an olive tree,
but only a deity would've known that this birth would be so
fruitful. We carry the names of gods, Alexander (defender
of mankind).

Little Boy as a House with Big Windows

My mother cries when she thinks of it.
The absorption of spirits.

But I think of it as an inheritance
of a large house

with big extravagant windows
to let all of the light flood in

to the soul.
Like when bits of my grandfather

flooded into my brother
and made a home there.

I assume the other bits of him are somewhere
wherever heaven is

rolling in a bed of purple hyacinths
or asking what my grandmother needs

from the store
still pushing grocery carts

through the clouds.
The other day, I saw my brother

biting into an unapologetically purple
eggplant and thought of his stubbornness.

This is how he will live longer than the rest of us
breaking bits off of ourselves

to feed to the living
dead.

Survival is a gruesome thing.
And I've seen it

in my grandmother's good eye
when she asks my mother to paint her room purple,

and my mother paints her room purple
like the hyacinths or the eggplants.

The only vegetable that my grandfather would eat,
but perhaps it was because of the color.

Today, I look at my brother,
picky with his food,

and think of that day in the grocery store
when my grandfather flooded into him

unapologetic
in his light.

VI. HOUSE OF THE MATERNAL

Cockpit

Sometimes, I think I could suffocate in this openness.
My mother slept in Puente De Jobos with nothing

but mosquito netting to protect her from the heat
and the dogs and all the dogs in heat. The mosquitos,

fat with my mother's blood, still flew in and out
of the holes in the netting. Even with those thick socks

pulled up to her knees, she couldn't stop the world
from picking at the flesh left exposed. I suppose

this is why I pull the sheets tight over my bare body
at night. I wrap myself like a basket of french bread

and pray the girls don't know the warm scent of
someone who is afraid of birth and sex and girls

who fight like bulls. The sheets, crisp, white napkins,
create a veil over my head. In Puente De Jobos,

they tie steel blades to the ankles of roosters just
to watch them kill each other. My mother tells me

this as she tosses some slaughtered bird in a bowl
of flour, squishing her fingers into the meaty parts.

The bird was an unveiled woman before it was a bird.
The woman was open before she was unveiled.

I imagine the roosters wrestling in a crowded ring
and think of the first time I was called a whore.

My mother admits she had been fed to the cockpit
too as she throws a battered leg into the frying pot.

The oil jumps up, leaving chestnut-colored burns
on the flesh of her wrists, but she just wipes

the grease away and coats another leg in flour
to feed to the bubbling.

Dreams Won't Feed You Forever

It is 3 a.m. now, and she hurdles her restless body over
the balcony like a single drop of rain—soars across

the Great Lakes with wings of a vulture and collapses
in her mother's kitchen. Her mother, frozen in time,

is in the same place she left her waiting. The girl cries,
because the kitchen is not real, and her mother

doesn't know about time travel. She sets guava pastries
on the dining table and rubs her swollen belly.

Tells her, her mouth swollen with tears, *take care*
of yourself, take care of your boys. Eat something other

than the flesh of your mother's ghost. Dreams won't
feed you forever. Forever asleep, she sips kale smoothies.

Swallows them like guava pastries until liquid fills her
rib cage. Spits out the bones of her mother, too tired

to cook. She lays on the ottoman like an empty dishwasher
ready to be filled. Too drained to take care of her boys,

let alone herself. Her body, a slip of paper never written
on. Her mother pulls her close, smears her forehead

with a powdered-sugar kiss, runs a cold thumb down her
spine. The kitchen's heart is pumping with flour and

music, and the boys twirl in circles around the dining
table, and they all know. The girl wakes to a phone call.

Marmalade

for R

I. Virgin Islands

On our last trip together, I am on a catamaran
with him and his family. We are both sprawled

out on this netting, the water splashing against
our backs, and a crew member offers us these

tiny sandwiches. He asks me to take a picture
of him, and when he isn't satisfied with the first,

he asks me to take another and another. I take
over a hundred pictures, but he claims, *each one*

looks like the embodiment of autism. He cries
as the boat pulls into the dock and says, *you'll find*

someone much better looking who doesn't have
Aspergers when you go to college. Because I love him,

I fear I will have to take care of him for the rest
of my life. My fear, a fat whale I hide in my gut.

II. Cherry Capital Airport

He says *old people look like snapping turtles*,
and I see us walking through the grocery store,

pushing our pudding-filled carts as if we are
wading through quicksand. For now, we push

only our suitcases, the planes landing on the
tarmac like snowflakes. Outside,

the cries of bluebirds rise above the coagulated
membrane of cherry trees.

III. Seaside, FL

He tells me to close my eyes and stick my hands
out, but this is my greatest fear. When I tell him

this, he laughs—says he wants a small wedding
in Vermont and three children. He tells me, *you*

shouldn't be afraid of small creatures, so I close
my eyes, make my hands a cradle to hold the ocean

until it's still. A clear marmalade slides through
my fingers, beautiful in its coldness. Later,

I will learn these were jellyfish eggs and remember
their arms that hung from their bodies like ruffled

skirts. The bridal gowns they will wear until they are
swallowed by something much bigger than them.

Jellyfish Wasteland

She leaves a scarlet love mark in the shape of one hundred rays bursting from the surface of my skin. My body, an instrument for her to play. Her body resembling broken strings of a guitar, she hunts me by my vibrations. Her iridescent mouth hovering over me like a spacecraft about to land. My hair tentacles braided with hers, we waltz. I mouth *one, two, three*—bubbles escaping my lips, and we are immortal, floating with the comets.

metamorphosis

for Pampa (Grandpa/Papa)

my mother walks up to the casket pushes
through the bodies places a domino on his chest
the Puerto Rican flag side up a dull red
the flash of a coqui frog's tongue the man
with the ponytail kisses his cheek before he leaves
with my mother's skin shedded and a little
boy plucks the strings of a guitar somewhere
an iguana is hatching a granddaughter strokes
a wooden bullfrog's spine a granddaughter spooning
the sky in the corner of a cracked house behind
a cracked door fragments of a granddaughter play
a tambourine her blessed tongue bleeding
terracotta tapped by the wings of a monarch butterfly
somewhere within the veins of banana plants
corpses sing to their daughters

so i let you be a canvas

for Alexander, my little brother

we are placed in a landscape where the only constant is you
and your curiosity   and tonight we are at the fair   you say
the sky is like cotton candy   so i try to break off a piece
of the clouds and feed it to you   you don't like the taste

of sugar crystals   how they evaporate once they are consumed
so i try to lend you bits   of myself instead   teach you how
to read and write and place my jacket on your bare shoulders
but the world is too big to stuff all   into your mouth

at once and you never liked literature so i show you   the fair
an array of lights to suit your colorful   palette paint to splash
onto your perfect face   you want to be a pirate   so i let you
be a canvas   soak into the landscape   the painted faces   hotdog

stands   people selling whatever they can   get their hands on
and i can't help but think   they want to get their hands on *you*
want to sell you in their stands   package you for delivery
to an unfamiliar face and it is this that frightens me   you

running into someone's arms   maybe a spouse or a friend's
but   not mine the day will come   when you are no longer
mine   but tonight we are at the fair   and the clouds are too
dilated to see beyond   the top of the circus   tents

the entertainers we spin each   other round in teacups until
your little stomach is flipped inside   out until   your perfect
face is streaked   with paint running i should've known
shouldn't have given you   so much sugar

shouldn't have let you be a canvas

—

we have spun into a different landscape now wet   and muggy
a barbeque at our neighbor's pool   where children whip past
me   and you don't want to wear your floaties   so i let you run
with the other children   watch you run away from me   your little

feet wrinkled like a chocolate date   back braised like a piglet
marinating   browned in the sun i wait to see your little face
your flushed cheeks full   of watermelon slices   juice dripping
down your chin   you always liked to run so i let you   barefoot

on the hot pool deck   i am offered a strawberry daiquiri
from a pregnant woman so i take it   sip the clouds through
a curly straw until   the landscape sways back and forth until
i see you run further from me   i see you in groups

of three and everything is a dream   the pregnant woman
all of the children running   their faces melt to the bottom
of my strawberry   daiquiri and i am slowly spinning it all
happens so   slowly as if i could've stopped it   stopped you

from diving into the pool without   your floaties   but nobody
was watching and everybody was running   to a destination
that could've waited   running to take the meat off   the grill
running to lather their wet bodies   in sunscreen the people

were spinning and i was spinning with them in a twisted
landscape where i existed without   you didn't see you falling
down beneath the surface   struggling to keep your little head
above the water   how could i have known you were struggling

in the midst of a beautiful frame

—

in the heart of a department store   i find myself in a different
landscape   i find you alive   touch my solid hands to your solid
face   thankful that someone pulled you out   of the water
maybe a spouse or a friend   and finally i wonder if i am still

dreaming   still pushing grocery carts through the clouds full
of rainwater   you want to see the action figures   want to run
through the aisles piled high with pumpkins   this is your favorite
time of year   when chrysanthemums bloom   when we go

shopping for pumpkins you choose the bluest ones   say blue
makes for the best canvas   because it is the color of   dreams
to carve its flesh would be to scratch the cornea of the world
to dig your hands into a cenote and pull out   pumpkin seeds

and now you are running   you want to see the action figures
but i am still carving our landscape   the children that roll
by in grocery carts   the mothers with their grocery lists   full
of items that are bound to be depleted   their grocery carts

a womb kicking   asking to be fed   rolling down an infinite
circuit where i am always depleted   where you are always
hungry   i am still rolling further into the clouds   full
of rainwater   so saturated with blue that you are nowhere

to be seen   your flushed cheeks   your perfect face a drop
in the bucket of the ocean   of someone else's grocery cart
i have lost   you and the crowds are too dense to see beyond
their painted faces   and it is this that truly frightens me   you

falling so far into the clouds that all i see is you   when i look
up   peering through a kaleidoscope   of gods

Notes

“Ken-ya See Us Now” quotes Season 10, Episode 9 of *Curb Your Enthusiasm* (one of my favorite shows). The line “I support Black and shit” is taken from the scene where Larry David and Leon are sitting on the couch watching basketball and eating licorice. Larry notices that Leon has been eating black licorice instead of red licorice and says, “I haven’t seen you take one piece of red licorice yet. Only black for you?” To which Leon responds, “Is there something wrong with a person supporting black and shit? Black licorice. Black jelly beans. Fucking blackouts.”

“the performance” references Saartjie Baartman, who was also commonly referred to as the Hottentot Venus. Saartjie Baartman was a South African woman who was exhibited as a freak show attraction in Europe during the 19th century due to her steatopygia. She is one of the first Black women known to be subjugated to human sex trafficking. *The New York Times* article “A Life Exposed” quotes Rachel Holmes, a professor at the University of London, who states that Baartman was “a symbol of the alienation and degradations of colonization, lost children, exile, the expropriation of female labor and the sexual and economic exploitation of black women by men, white and black.” After Baartman’s death, her sexual organs were on display for 150 years in the Musée de l'Homme. In 1994, Nelson Mandela requested that her remains be repatriated, and the French government finally agreed to return them to South Africa for a proper burial in 2002.

“the performance” quotes Megan Thee Stallion’s song “Body” from her album *Good News*.

“After the Song” is in conversation with Brigit Pegeen Kelly’s poem “Song.”

The title “athena as villanelle" was inspired by the fictional character Villanelle from the TV show *Killing Eve*, where Villanelle is a psychopathic assassin.

About the Author

Athena Nassar is an Egyptian-American poet, essayist, and short story writer from Atlanta, Georgia. She is an Interlochen Arts Academy alum and is currently an undergraduate student at Emerson College, where she is the head poetry editor of *The Emerson Review*. She is the recipient of the 2019 Scholastic National Gold Medal Portfolio Award, the 2021 San Miguel Writers' Conference Writing Contest, and the 2021 Academy of American Poets College Prize, among other honors. Her work has appeared in *Academy of American Poets, The Missouri Review, Southern Humanities Review, The Chattahoochee Review, Salt Hill, Lake Effect, New Orleans Review, Zone 3, Sequestrum, The Los Angeles Review, PANK,* and elsewhere.

Other Sundress Titles

Kneel Said the Night
Margo Berdeshevsky
$20

In Stories We Thunder
V. Ruiz
$16

Slack Tongue City
Mackenzie Berry
$16

Sweetbitter
Stacey Balkun
$16

Cosmobiological
Jilly Dreadful
$20

Dad Jokes from Late in the Patriarchy
Amorak Huey
$16

What Nothing
Anna Meister
$16

Hood Criatura
féi hernandez
$16

Nocturne in Joy
Tatiana Johnson-Boria
$16

the Colored page
Matthew E. Henry
$16

Year of the Unicorn Kidz
jason b. Crawford
$16

Something Dark to Shine In
Inès Pujos
$16

Slaughter the One Bird
Kimberly Ann Priest
#16

The Valley
Esteban Rodriguez
$16

To Everything There Is
Donna Vorreyer
$16

nightsong
Ever Jones
$16

CPSIA information can be obtained
at www.ICGtesting.com
Printed in the USA
JSHW021129120623
43031JS00004B/217

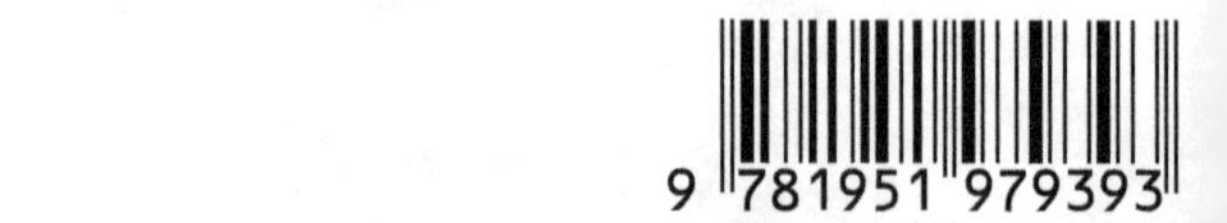